W9-AQT-331

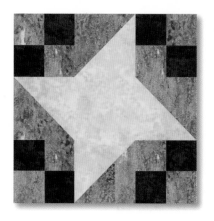

50 STATES QUILT BLOCKS
by Rita Weiss & Linda Causee

Before You Start

Choose the block you want to make. Inside this book, you will find a self-loading CD that contains the 50 state quilt block patterns in 5 different sizes. The files on the CD are easily opened using Adobe® Reader®. If you don't have Adobe® Reader® on your computer you can get a free download at http://www.adobe.com/. The site provides easy, step-by-step instructions for the download.

When you are ready to make your quilt, simply print out the required templates of your choice. Then glue the templates on to plastic or heavy cardboard. When you are certain that your glue has dried, cut out your templates. If your templates become worn, simply repeat the process.

Contents

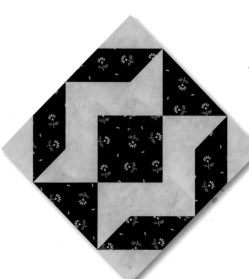

LEISURE ARTS, INC.
Maumelle, Arkansas

Produced by

Production Team

Creative Directors:	Jean Leinhauser and Rita Weiss
Photography:	Carol Wilson Mansfield
Book Design:	Linda Causee
Technical Editor:	Ann Harnden

Published by Leisure Arts

© 2014 by Leisure Arts, Inc.
104 Champs Blvd., STE 100
Maumelle, AR 72113-6738

www.leisurearts.com

All rights reserved. This publication is protected under federal copyright laws. Reproduction or distribution of this publication or any other Leisure Arts publication, including publications which are out of print, is prohibited unless specifically authorized. This includes, but is not limited to, any form of reproduction or distribution on or through the Internet, including posting, scanning, or e-mail transmission.

We have made every effort to ensure that these instructions are accurate and complete. We cannot, however, be responsible for human error, typographical mistakes, or variations in individual work.

Library of Congress Control Number: 2013952255

ISBN-13: 978-1-4647-1240-1

Introduction

Over 100 years ago, a popular farm magazine, **Hearth and Home**, began a series of state quilt blocks. They invited readers from all over the country to send in actual pieced blocks that would represent their state. At the time, there were only 48 states in the United States, and within five years, the magazine had collected and printed 48 blocks.

Eventually the magazine held another contest asking for blocks for "outlying territories. " This series produced blocks for Alaska and Hawaii to complete today's 50 states.

The magazine continued publishing other quilt blocks for the next 20 years before it ceased publication. Because the magazine was printed on newsprint and not intended for posterity, few copies still survive, and there are very few complete copies of the entire state collection. Over the years, however, many quilters have paid homage to a particular state by creating their own state quilt block.

As we have traveled and moved around the country, we have always wanted to collect other quilt blocks honoring those states that were meaningful to us. Eventually we decided rather than picking and choosing which states to honor, we would create our own collection of 50 quilt blocks.

And, just to make things more interesting, we decided to make some quilts using these blocks. Linda got to work immediately and quickly made three quilts. The first one, a small wall hanging on page 55, celebrates the state where she was born. The second one, on page 57, commemorates her family's visit to Alaska, while her third quilt, on page 59, is made up of blocks from many states she has visited.

Rita, on the other hand, concentrated on telling the story of her life in one quilt, on page 61.

Now you can tell your own story in quilts. Whether you are an experienced quilter or just a beginner, one of the most difficult parts of the project often is finding the necessary templates. This book and its enclosed CD can solve that problem. Just place the CD into your computer, click on the state block of your choice in the size you desire and print out all the templates you will need for your quilt.

If you've forgotten—or if you've never learned—how to make a quilt, we've included some basic directions on the CD.

So make a queen-size bed quilt, a lap quilt, a wall hanging or a miniature quilt. All of the necessary templates are just a click away.

Alabama **Rambler**

Templates and Fabric

8 K triangles, dk fabric
8 K triangles, med fabric
16 P triangles, lt fabric
4 N squares, dk fabric
4 N squares, med fabric
8 N squares, lt fabric

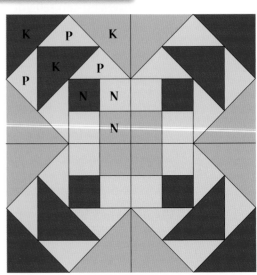

Alaska **North Star**

Templates and Fabric

4 C triangles, lt fabric
2 C triangles, dk fabric
2 C triangles, med fabric
20 D triangles, dk fabric
20 D triangles, med fabric
4 E squares, lt fabric

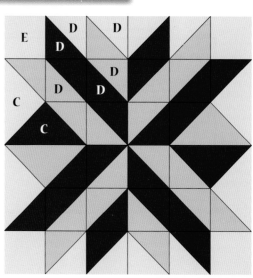

Arizona **Cactus Flower**

Templates and Fabric

1 A square, very dk fabric
20 D triangles, med fabric
20 D triangles, lt fabric
4 E squares, lt fabric
4 F strips, dk fabric

Arkansas Snowflake

Templates and Fabric

4 A squares, lt fabric
2 C triangles, dk fabric
2 C triangles, med fabric
2 G triangles, med fabri
2 G triangles, dk fabric
8 H triangles, lt fabric

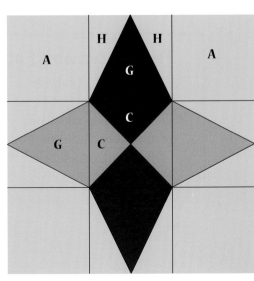

Road to *California*

Templates and Fabric

2 A squares, lt fabric
4 B triangles, lt fabric
4 B triangles, dk fabric
6 E squares, lt fabric
6 E squares, dk fabric

Colorado **Beauty**

Templates and Fabric

12 K triangles, lt fabric
16 K triangles, med fabric
4 K triangles, dk fabric

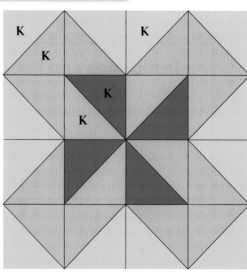

9

Connecticut

Mosaic

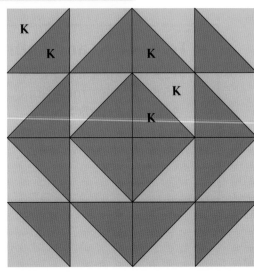

Templates and Fabric

16 K triangles, lt fabric
16 K triangles, dk fabric

Delaware

Sea Pine

Templates and Fabric

4 C triangles, blue fabric
14 D triangles, blue fabric
3 D triangles, very dk green fabric
7 D triangles, dk green fabric
7 D triangles, med green fabric
4 D triangles, lt green fabric
3 D triangles, brown fabric
4 E squares, blue fabric
1 E square, brown fabric
4 F strips, blue fabric

Florida **Sunshine**

Templates and Fabric

4 K triangles, dk fabric
4 K triangles, lt fabric
28 M triangles, lt fabric
24 M triangles, med fabric
4 M triangles, dk fabric
4 N squares, med fabric
8 N squares, lt fabric
2 O strips, dk fabric

Georgia

Love Chain

Templates and Fabric

2 L squares, med fabric
44 M triangles, lt fabric
24 M triangles, med fabric
20 M triangles, dk fabric
12 N squares, lt fabric

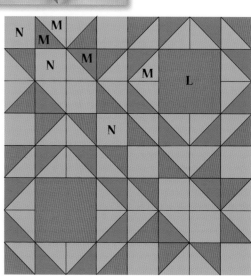

Hawaii Sun

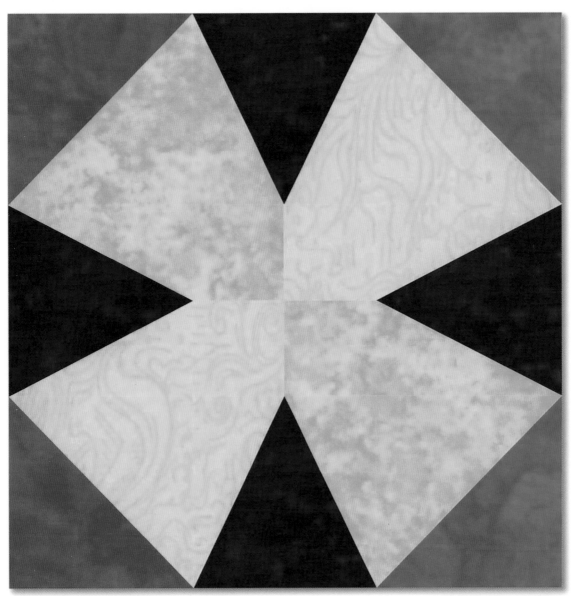

Templates and Fabric

4 B triangles, dk fabric
2 B triangles, med fabric
2 B triangles, lt fabric
2 E squares, med fabric
2 E squares, lt fabric
4 G triangles, very dk fabric
4 H triangles, med fabric
4 H triangles, lt fabric

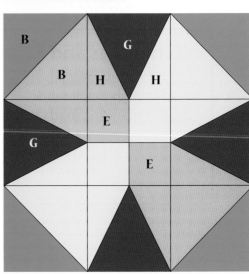

Idaho **Beauty**

Templates and Fabric

4 L squares, dk fabric
32 M triangles, lt fabric
32 M triangles, dk fabric
12 N squares, lt fabric

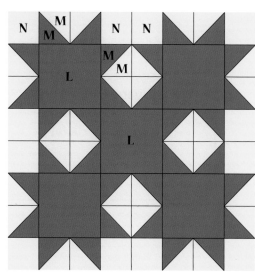

Illinois

Windy City

Templates and Fabric

1 A square, med fabric
8 E squares, med fabric
12 H triangles, lt fabric
12 H triangles, dk fabric

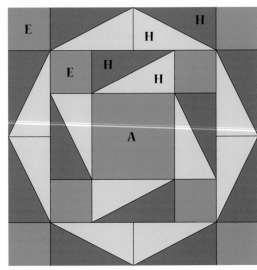

Indiana Puzzle

Templates and Fabric

1 A square, lt fabric
4 C Triangles, lt fabric
4 C Triangles, med fabric
8 E squares, med fabric
8 E squares, dk fabric

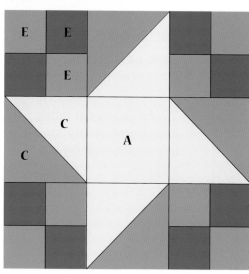

17

Iowa **Corn**

Templates and Fabric

1 L square, lt fabric
32 M triangles, med fabric
8 M triangles, dk fabric
24 M triangles, lt fabric
8 N squares, med fabric
8 N squares, dk fabric
12 N squares, lt fabric

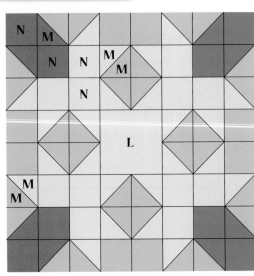

Kansas **Star**

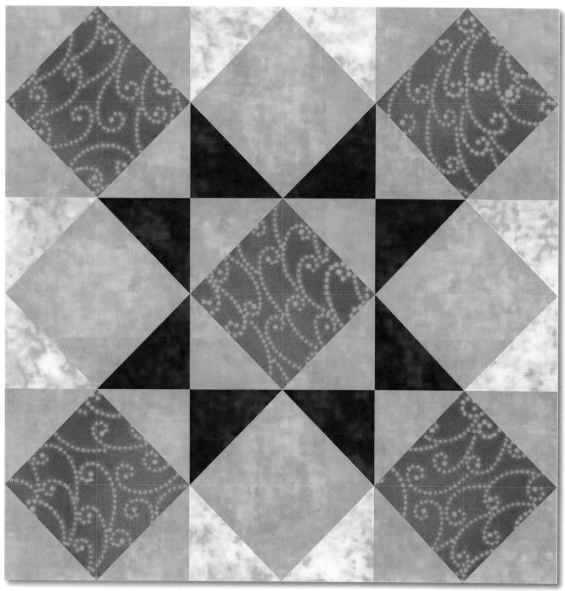

Templates and Fabric

8 D triangles, very dk fabric
20 D triangles, dk fabric
8 D triangles, lt fabric
36 D triangles, med fabric

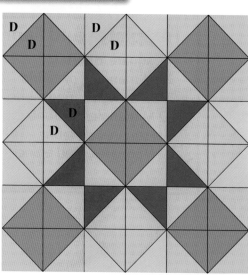

Kentucky Chain

Templates and Fabric

1 L square, dk fabric
24 M triangles, dk fabric
24 M triangles, med fabric
32 M triangles, lt fabric
8 N squares, dk fabric
12 N squares, med fabric

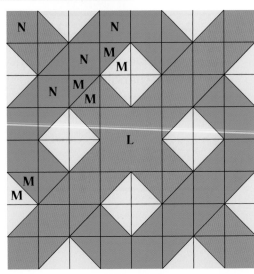

Louisiana **Star**

Templates and Fabric

8 K triangles, dk fabric
8 K triangles, med fabric
8 K triangles, lt fabric
4 L squares, lt fabric

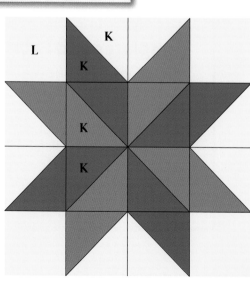

Maine **Woods**

Templates and Fabric

4 C triangles, lt fabric
6 C triangles, very dk fabric
4 D triangles, lt fabric
12 D triangles, med fabric
4 D triangles, very dk fabric
8 D triangles, dk fabric
4 E squares, very dk fabric
4 F strips, med fabric

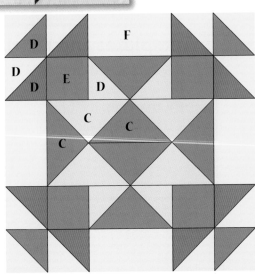

Maryland

Bell

Templates and Fabric

8 B triangles, med fabric
20 D triangles, dk fabric
4 D triangles, lt fabric
32 I triangles, lt fabric

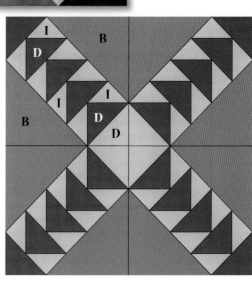

Massachusetts

Star

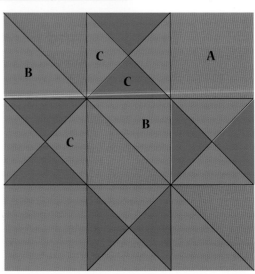

Templates and Fabric

1 A square, med fabric
1 A square, lt fabric
3 B triangles, med fabric
3 B triangles, lt fabric
8 C triangles, lt fabric
8 C triangles, dk fabric

Michigan **Beauty**

Templates and Fabric

1 A square, lt fabric
24 D triangles, lt fabric
24 D triangles, dk fabric
4 E squares, lt fabric
4 E squares, dk fabric

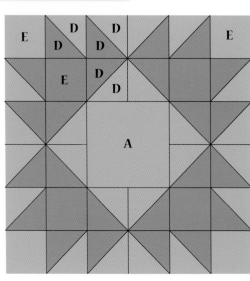

Minnesota **Diamonds**

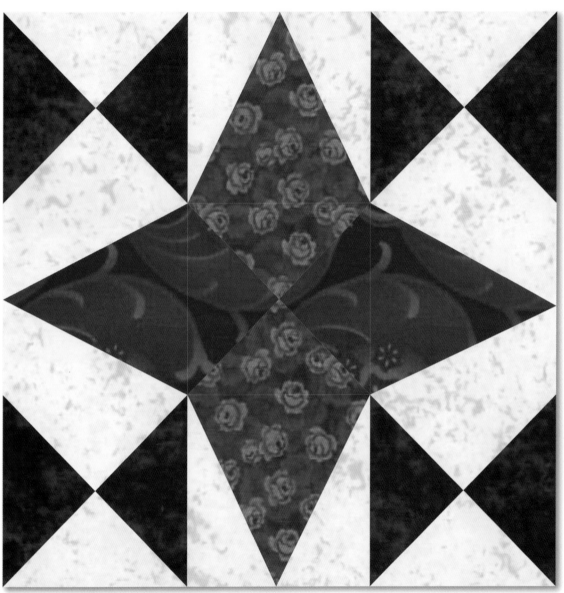

Templates and Fabric

8 C triangles, lt fabric
8 C triangles, very dk fabric
2 C triangles, dk fabric
2 C triangles, med fabric
2 G triangles, dk fabric
2 G triangles, med fabric
8 H triangles, lt fabric

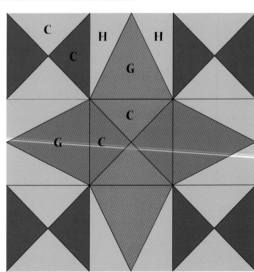

Mississippi Star

Templates and Fabric

- 4 C triangles, dk fabric
- 8 C triangles, lt fabric
- 12 D triangles, dk fabric
- 12 D triangles, med fabric
- 4 E squares, lt fabric
- 16 I triangles, med fabric
- 16 I triangles, lt fabric

Missouri Windmill

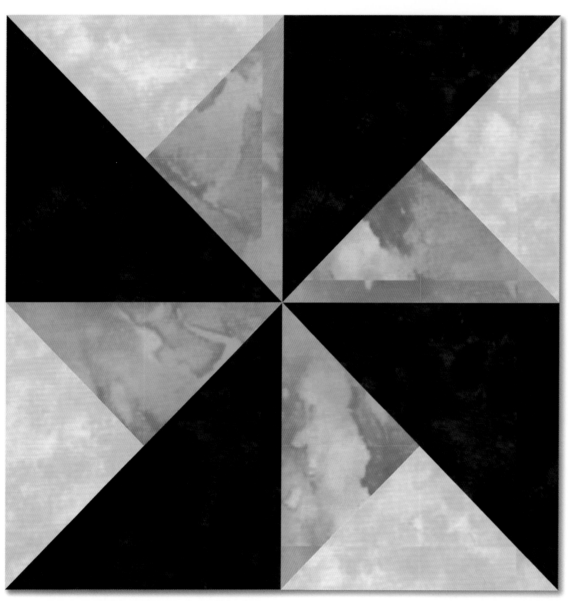

Templates and Fabric

4 J triangles, dk fabric
8 K triangles, med fabric
8 K triangles, lt fabric

Montana Maze

Templates and Fabric

- 4 B triangles, med fabric
- 4 B triangles, lt fabric
- 4 C triangles, med fabric
- 8 D triangles, very dk fabric
- 2 E squares, lt fabric
- 2 E squares, dk fabric
- 4 F strips, very dk fabric

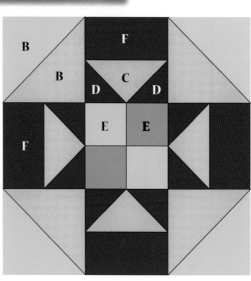

Nebraska **Diamonds**

Templates and Fabric

8 C triangles, dk fabric
2 C triangles, lt fabric
4 C triangles, med fabric
8 D triangles, very dk fabric
16 D triangles, lt fabric
4 D triangles, dk fabric
4 F strips, dk fabric

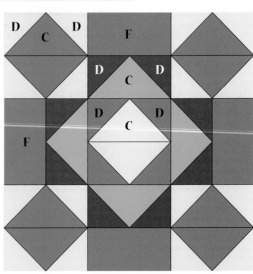

Nevada

Nine Patch

Templates and Fabric

4 A squares, dk fabric
16 D triangles, lt fabric
4 E squares, lt fabric
2 E squares, med fabric
2 E squares, very dk fabric
16 I triangles, very dk fabric

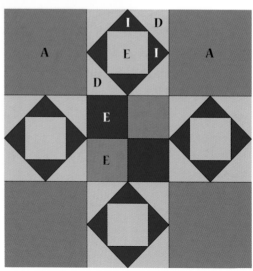

New Hampshire

Granite

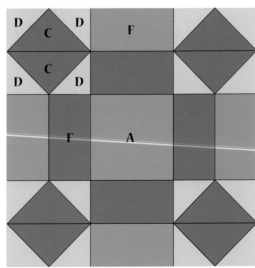

Templates and Fabric

1 A square, med fabric
8 C squares, dk fabric
16 D triangles, lt fabric
4 F strips, dk fabric
4 F strips, med fabric

New Jersey

Chevrons

Templates and Fabric

36 D triangles, lt fabric
36 D triangles, dk fabric

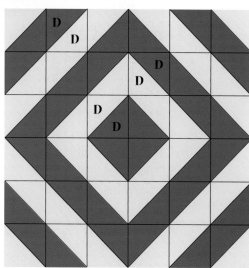

New Mexico

Sun Rays

Templates and Fabric

1 A square, lt fabric
20 D triangles, lt fabric
8 D triangles, med fabric
4 D triangles, dk fabric
4 E squares, med fabric
4 F strips, dk fabric
8 I triangles, med fabric
8 I triangles, dk fabric

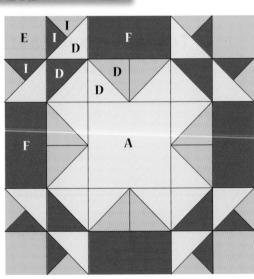

New York

Empire State

Templates and Fabric

16 K triangles, lt fabric
16 K triangles, dk fabric

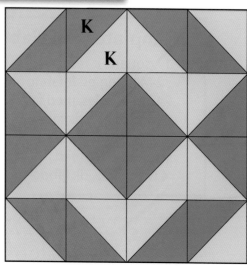

North Carolina

Lilies

Templates and Fabric

1 L square, lt fabric
32 M triangles, lt fabric
24 M triangles, med fabric
8 M triangles, dk fabric
12 N squares, lt fabric
12 N squares, med fabric
4 N squares, dk fabric

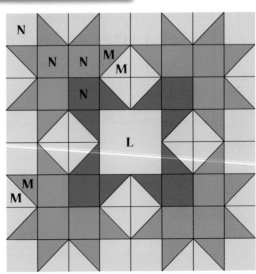

North Dakota

Star

Templates and Fabric

4 B triangles, dk fabric
4 B triangles, very dk fabric
4 D triangles, dk fabric
4 D triangles, med fabric
4 H triangles, dk fabric
4 H triangles, med fabric
8 H triangles, lt fabric

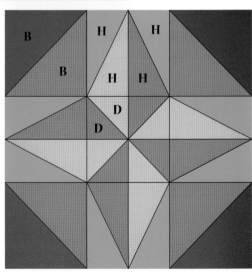

Ohio **Star**

Templates and Fabric

4 A squares, lt fabric
1 A square, dk fabric
8 C triangles, med fabric
4 C triangles, lt fabric
4 C triangles, dk fabric

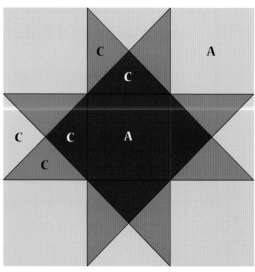

Road to *Oklahoma*

Templates and Fabric

4 K triangles, med fabric
4 K triangles, lt fabric
2 L squares, med fabric
6 L squares, lt fabric
4 L squares, dk fabric

Oregon
Fir Tree

Templates and Fabric

2 A squares, lt blue
1 A square, brown
2 B triangles, lt blue
1 C triangle, very lt green
2 D triangles, lt green
2 D triangles, dk green
2 D triangles, very dk green
4 D triangles, lt blue
1 F strip, lt green
2 F strips, dk green
2 F strips, very dk green
2 F strips, lt blue

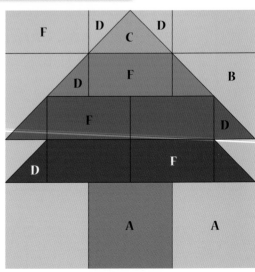

Pennsylvania Crossroads

Templates and Fabric

2 L squares, dk fabric
2 L squares, lt fabric
32 M triangles, dk fabric
32 M triangles, lt fabric
8 N squares, dk fabric
8 N squares, lt fabric

Rhode Island

Red Maple

Templates and Fabric

4 K triangles, dk fabric
1 L square, lt fabric
16 M triangles, dk fabric
24 M triangles, med fabric
16 M triangles, lt fabric
12 N squares, lt fabric
4 N squares, med fabric
8 P triangles, lt fabric

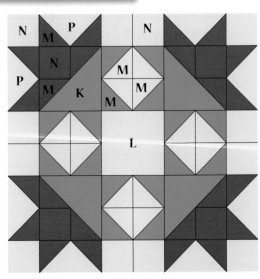

South Carolina

Star

Templates and Fabric

8 C triangles, very dk fabric
8 C triangles, lt fabric
20 D triangles, lt fabric
5 E squares, dk fabric
20 I triangles, med fabric

South Dakota

Gold

Templates and Fabric

5 A squares, dk fabric
8 D triangles, very dk fabric
8 D triangles, very light fabric
8 D triangles, light fabric
4 E squares, med fabric

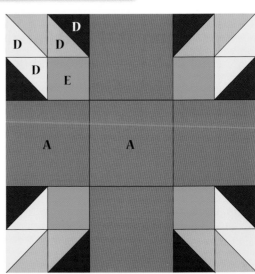

Tennessee Waltz

Templates and Fabric

8 E squares, very lt fabric
10 E squares, lt fabric
2 E squares, dk fabric
4 G triangles, light fabric
8 H triangles, dk fabric

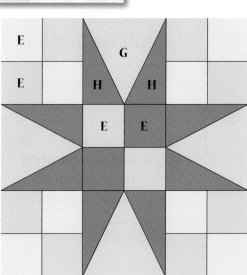

Texas Patriot

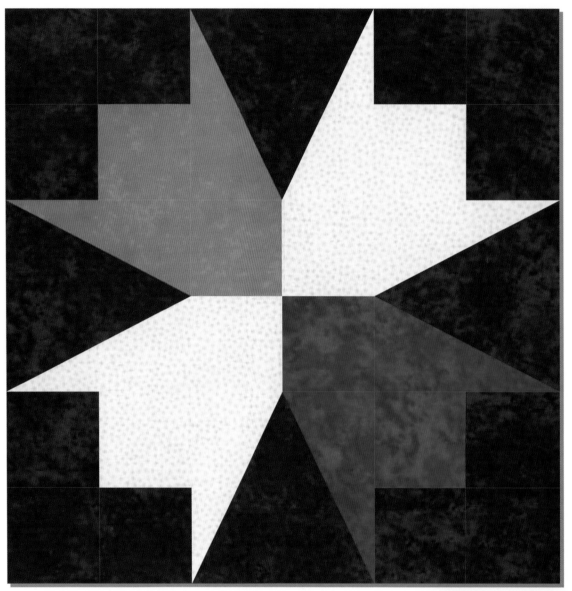

Templates and Fabric

12 E squares, very dk fabric
2 E squares, med fabric
2 E squares, dk fabric
4 E squares, lt fabric
4 G triangles, very dk fabric
2 H triangles, med fabric
2 H triangles, dk fabric
4 H triangles, lt fabric

Utah **Salt Lake**

Templates and Fabric

- 12 K triangles, dk fabric
- 4 K triangles, med fabric
- 8 P triangles, lt fabric
- 8 P triangles, med fabric
- 4 L squares, lt fabric

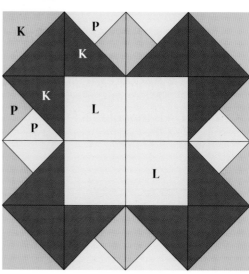

Vermont

Maple Leaf

Templates and Fabric

1 A square, dk fabric
2 A squares, lt fabric
2 A squares, med fabric
4 B triangles, lt fabric
4 B triangles, med fabric

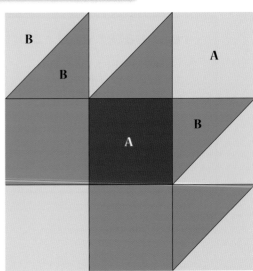

Virginia Reel

Templates and Fabric

2 J triangles, lt fabric
2 J triangles, dk fabric
6 K triangles, lt fabric
6 K triangles, dk fabric
4 P triangles, lt fabric
4 P triangles, dk fabric

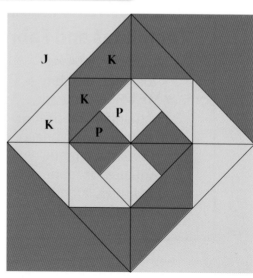

Washington

Pine

Templates and Fabric

5 K triangles, lt fabric
2 K triangles, dk fabric
27 M triangles, lt fabric
31 M triangles, med fabric
4 M triangles, dk fabric
16 N squares, lt fabric
2 N squares, dk fabric
2 Q triangles, lt fabric
2 Q triangles, dk fabric

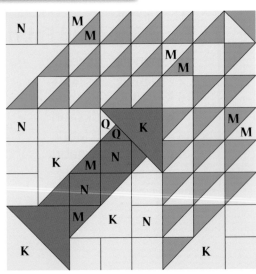

West Virginia

Bell

Templates and Fabric

16 K triangles, dk fabric
16 K triangles, lt fabric

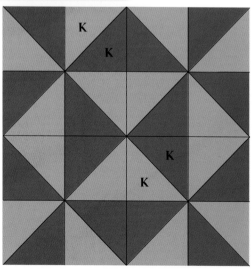

51

Wisconsin Dells

Templates and Fabric

4 B triangles, dk fabric
8 D triangles, med fabric
12 D triangles, lt fabric
1 E square, med fabric
8 H triangles, lt fabric
8 H triangles, dk fabric
4 I triangles, dk fabric

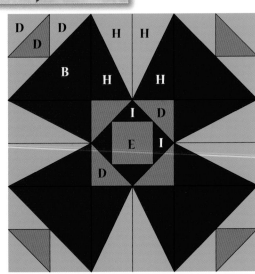

Wyoming **Star**

Templates and Fabric

16 D triangles, very dk fabric
4 D triangles, dk fabric
12 D triangles, med fabric
32 D triangles, lt fabric
4 E squares, lt fabric

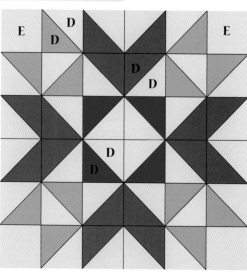

Born in Indiana

Celebrate your home state with its state block!

APPROXIMATE SIZE
24" x 24"

BLOCK SIZE
6" x 6" square (finished)

TEMPLATES NEEDED
A Square (6")
C Triangle (6")
E Square (6")

MATERIALS
$1/4$ yd off-white
$1/2$ yd light blue
$1/4$ yd dark blue
26" square batting
$3/4$ yd backing
$1/4$ yd binding

CUTTING

Blocks

9 A Squares, off-white
36 C Triangles, off-white
36 C Triangles, light blue
72 E squares, light blue
72 E Squares, dark blue

Finishing

4 strips, $1^1/2$" x $18^1/2$", dark blue
   (first border)
4 strips, $2^1/2$" x $20^1/2$", light blue
   (second border)
3 strips, $2^1/2$"-wide, light blue
   (binding)

Instructions

1. Make 9 Indiana Puzzle blocks.

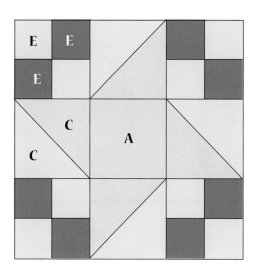

2. Sew the blocks together in three rows of three blocks.

3. Sew the rows together.

4. Refer to General Directions on the enclosed CD, to finish your quilt.

Memories of Alaska

What better way to remember a cruise to Alaska than a quilt using the Alaska North Star block and alternating it with some memorable photos.

APPROXIMATE SIZE
37" x 55"

BLOCK SIZE
9" x 9" square (finished)

TEMPLATES NEEDED
C Triangle (9")
D Triangle
E Square

MATERIALS

Alaska Blocks
$1/2$ yd white
1 yd light blue
1 yd dark blue

Photo Blocks
*$7/8$ yd white fabric or 12 prepared fabric sheets

Finishing
60" batting
$3^1/2$ yds backing
$1/4$ yd binding

CUTTING

Alaska North Star Blocks
32 E squares, white
32 C triangles, white
64 D triangles, white
16 C triangles, lt blue
160 D triangles, lt blue
16 C triangles, dk blue
160 D triangles, dk blue

Photo Blocks
*7 photos, $5^1/2$" x $5^1/2$"
14 strips, $2^1/2$" x $5^1/2$", light blue
14 strips, $2^1/2$" x $9^1/2$", light blue

*Size your photos to finish 5" square (cut $5^1/2$" square).

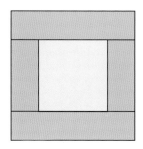

Finishing
4 strips, $4^1/2$"-wide strips, white (first border)
4 strips, $2^1/2$"-wide, light blue (binding)

Instructions

1. Make 8 Alaska North Star blocks using the 9" templates found on the CD.

2. Choose 7 of your favorite photos. Refer to How to Print Photos to Fabric on the enclosed CD and print photos to fabric. Trim to $5^1/2$" x $5^1/2$". Sew $2^1/2$" x $5^1/2$" light blue strips to opposite sides of the photo; sew $2^1/2$" x $9^1/2$" light blue strips to top and bottom.

3. Arrange Alaska North Star Block and Photo blocks in five rows of three blocks.

4. Sew the blocks together in rows, then sew rows together

5. Refer to General Directions on the enclosed CD, to finish your quilt.

States I've Visited

Why not make a quilt with a collection of the states you've visited during your lifetime?

APPROXIMATE SIZE
63" x 78"

BLOCK SIZE
12" x 12" square (finished)

TEMPLATES NEEDED
A Square
B Triangle
C Triangle
D Triangle
E Square
G Triangle
H Triangle
H rev Triangle
I Triangle
J Triangle
K Triangle
M Triangle
N Square
O Strip
P Triangle

MATERIALS
1 yard each of blue, green, light orange,
dark orange, yellow, white, black (blocks)
2 yards print (sashing)
1/4 yard blue (cornerstones)
1/2 yard binding
full-size batting
4 yards backing

CUTTING

Alaska North Star Blocks
4 E squares, white
4 C triangles, white
8 D triangles, white
2 C triangles, blue
20 D triangles, blue
2 C triangles, green
20 D triangles, green

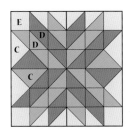

Michigan Beauty
1 A square, green
24 D triangles, green
24 D triangles, blue
4 E squares, green
4 E squares, blue

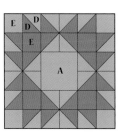

Road to California
2 A squares, white
4 B triangles, white
4 B triangles, blue
6 E squares, green
6 E squares, blue

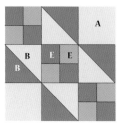

Florida Sunshine
4 K triangles, dk orange
4 K triangles yellow
28 M triangles, yellow
24 M triangles, lt orange
4 M triangles, dk orange
4 N squares, lt orange
8 N squares, yellow
2 O strips, dk orange

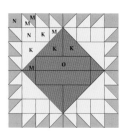

Illinois Windy City
1 A square, green
8 E squares, green
12 H triangles, green
12 H triangles, blue

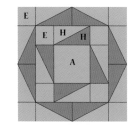

Indiana Puzzle

1 A square, yellow
4 C triangles, yellow
4 C triangles, green
8 E squares, green
8 E squares, blue

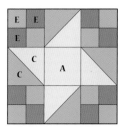

Maryland Bell

8 B triangles, dk orange
20 D triangles, black
4 D triangles, lt orange
32 I triangles, lt orange

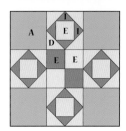

Nevada Nine Patch

4 A squares, green
16 D triangles, white
4 E squares, white
2 E squares, yellow
2 E squares, blue
16 I triangles, blue

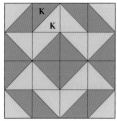

New York Empire State

16 K triangles, lt orange
16 K triangles, blue

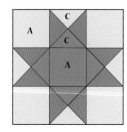

Ohio Star

4 A squares, white
1 A square, blue
8 C triangles, dk orange
4 C triangles, blue
4 C triangles, white

Texas Patriot

12 E squares, black
2 E squares, blue
2 E squares, dk orange
4 E squares, white
4 G triangles, black
2 H* triangles, blue
2 H* triangles, red
4 H triangles, white
*1 H triangle is reversed

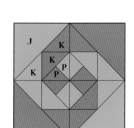

Virginia Reel

2 J triangles, green
2 J triangles, dk orange
6 K triangles, green
6 K triangles, dk orange
4 P triangles, green
4 P triangles, dk orange

Finishing

31 strips, 3½" x 12½", print (sashing)
12 squares, 3½" x 3½", blue (cornerstones)
7 strips, 3½"-wide, print (border)
8 strips, 2½"-wide, blue (binding)

Instructions

1. Make one block of each of 12 different blocks.

2. Arrange blocks, sashing strips and cornerstones in rows.

3. Sew block rows together in rows with sashing strips in between. Sew sashing and cornerstone rows.

4. Sew block and sashing rows together.

5. Refer to General Directions on the enclosed CD, to finish your quilt.

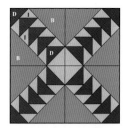

The Quilt of My Life

Start in the center with the Ohio and Florida blocks, the birthplaces of husband and wife, surround them with the New York block which is where they met, add the Vermont blocks where they spent their honeymoon. Create a border of the California block where they have spent most of their married life with two Illinois blocks to remind them of special friends.

APPROXIMATE SIZE
95" x "113

BLOCK SIZE
15" x 15" square (finished)

TEMPLATES NEEDED
A Square
B Triangle
C Triangle
E Square
H Triangle
K Triangle
M Triangle
N Square
O Rectangle

MATERIALS
1 yard each of light blue, medium blue, dark blue, light green, medium green, dark green, red, orange, yellow, beige (blocks)
3 yards floral (sashing, border)
1/2 yard binding
queen-size batting
queen-size backing

CUTTING

Road to California
2 A squares, yellow
4 B triangles, yellow
4 B triangles, med blue
6 E squares, lt blue
6 E squares, med blue

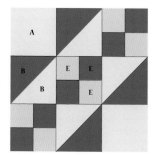

Florida Sunshine
4 K triangles, red
4 K triangles, yellow
28 M triangles, yellow
24 M triangles, orange
4 M triangles, red
4 N squares, orange
8 N squares, yellow
2 O strips, red

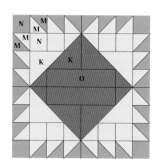

Illinois Windy City
1 A square, green
8 E squares, green
*12 H triangles, yellow
*12 H triangles, blue

*4 H triangles are reversed.

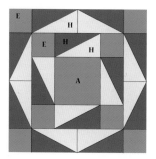

New York Empire State
16 K triangles, orange
16 K triangles, dark blue

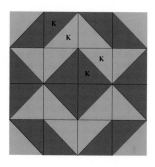

Ohio Star

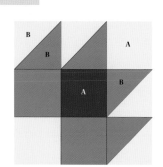

4 A squares, off white
1 A square, dark blue
8 C triangles, red
4 C triangles, off white
4 C triangles, dark blue

Vermont Maple Leaf

1 A square, dark green
2 A squares, light green
2 A squares, medium green
4 B triangles, light green
4 B triangles, medium green

Finishing

49 strips, 2¹/₂" x 15¹/₂", floral (sashing)
20 squares, 2¹/₂" x 2¹/₂", red (cornerstones
8 strips, 4¹/₂"-wide, floral (border)
4 strips, 2¹/₂"-wide, red
  (binding)

Instructions

Note: *There are a total of 30 blocks in this quilt, but only 6 different state blocks. Use any combination of blocks for your own unique quilt.*

1. Make 30 blocks of your choice.

2. Arrange blocks and sashing strips in rows.

3. Sew block rows together in rows with sashing strips in between. Sew sashing strips in between rows.

4. Refer to General Directions on the enclosed CD, to finish your quilt.

Index